Carmit Rachel Swed

I Want to Stay in Kindergarten

Illustrated by: Racheli Ben Zeev

Carmit Rachel Swed
I Want to Stay in Kindergarten

All Rights Reserved
Copyright © 2024

Illustrations: Racheli Ben Zeev
Design and Graphics: Lior Naim
Translation and Editing: Dr. English

No part of this publication may be duplicated, reproduced, photographed, recorded, translated, stored in a retrieval system, or transmitted in any form or by any means, electronic, mechanical, recording, or otherwise, without the written consent of the authors. Any type of commercial use of the material in this book is strictly prohibited without the written consent of the authors.

To my daughter Emma,
who teaches me something new every day

Summer is here, and vacation starts soon.
Oh, what a feeling—we're all over the moon!
We'll soon have an end-of-the-year party,
and Mommy said: "Anna, we'll get a gift for Teacher Marty."

Suddenly, I realize what it means, and I get sad,
I'll say goodbye to the teacher and friends I had.
Goodbye to teacher Marty, and teacher Grace,
then put all the toys and games back in their place.

We won't arrange the chairs by the tables again,
and we won't eat our breakfast every morning at ten.
We won't go out to the backyard to run around,
and we'll only play in the town's playground.

Who will take care of our vegetable nooks?
Who will read all of our favorite books?
Who'll feed the parrot, and the colorful fish?
Who'll take care of our rabbit
and clean out his dish?

The paints, the brushes, all the scissors too,
are arranged in a line next to the bottles of glue.
All I want is to throw it all down to the floor,
and get myself dirty, and walk through the door,
and make a bigger mess than there ever was before.

I'm confused. What's happening to me?
One moment I feel sad, the next - filled with glee.
I won't see my teacher and all the friends I had,
but I'll have a new kindergarten, which makes me glad.

My head is spinning, and my tummy is sore.
Will I not see my kindergarten anymore?

Mommy says she understands, goodbyes really are hard,
and sometimes our feelings can catch us off guard.
It's okay to be scared and mad when things are done,
and it's also okay to smile, laugh and have fun.

"Don't worry," Mom says, "you'll have Alex and Jade.
And besides, if you miss all of it,
or just one specific part,
you can always remember,
it's right here in your heart."

Mommy says: "Now, close your eyes, dear.
You don't need to worry. Mommy's right here.
Whenever you feel afraid or in doubt,
just take three deep breaths;
three in, three out."

And then Mommy hugs me, close and tight,
and I feel my heart filling up with light.
I'll have tons of new friends; I feel no fear.
I smile a huge smile, from ear to ear.

www.ingramcontent.com/pod-product-compliance
Lightning Source LLC
LaVergne TN
LVRC090726070526
838199LV00019B/544